EASTER

FESTIVALS AROUND THE **WORLD**

Grace Jones

www.av2books.com

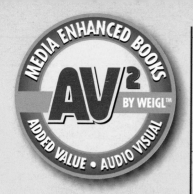

AV² provides enriched content that supplements and complements this book. Weigl's AV² books strive to create inspired learning and engage young minds in a total learning experience.

Your AV² Media Enhanced books come alive with...

Audio
Listen to sections of the book read aloud.

Key Words
Study vocabulary, and complete a matching word activity.

Go to **www.av2books.com**, and enter this book's unique code.

Video
Watch informative video clips.

Quizzes
Test your knowledge.

BOOK CODE

L B F 3 3 7 5 8

Embedded Weblinks
Gain additional information for research.

Slide Show
View images and captions, and prepare a presentation.

AV² by Weigl brings you media enhanced books that support active learning.

Try This!
Complete activities and hands-on experiments.

... and much, much more!

Published by AV² by Weigl
350 5ᵗʰ Avenue, 59ᵗʰ Floor New York, NY 10118
Website: www.av2books.com

Library of Congress Cataloging-in-Publication Data

Names: Jones, Grace, 1990- author.
Title: Easter / Grace Jones.
Description: New York : AV2 by Weigl, 2018. I Series: Festivals around the world
Identifiers: LCCN 2018003642 (print) I LCCN 2018005277 (ebook) I ISBN 9781489678218 (Multi User ebook) I ISBN 9781489678195 (hardcover : alk. paper) I ISBN 9781489678201 (softcover)
Subjects: LCSH: Easter--Juvenile literature.
Classification: LCC BV55 (ebook) I LCC BV55 .J66 2018 (print) I DDC 263/.93--dc23
LC record available at https://lccn.loc.gov/2018003642

Printed in the United States of America in Brainerd, Minnesota
1 2 3 4 5 6 7 8 9 0 22 21 20 19 18

032018
120417

Project Coordinator: Heather Kissock   Designer: Ana María Vidal

First published by Book Life in 2017

Weigl acknowledges Getty Images, Alamy, and iStock as the primary image suppliers for this title.

EASTER

FESTIVALS AROUND THE WORLD

Contents

Hello, my name is Sarah.

When you see Sarah, she will tell you how to say a word.

What Is a Festival?

A festival takes place when people come together to celebrate a special event or time of the year. Some festivals last for only one day and others can go on for many months.

Some people celebrate festivals by having a party with their family and friends. Others celebrate by holding special events, performing dances or playing music.

Sarah says:
BY-BULL (Bible)

6

What Is Christianity?

Christianity is a religion that began over two thousand years ago in the Middle East. Christians believe in one God and they pray to Him in a Christian place of worship, usually a church.

Christians read and learn from a holy book called the Bible. The Bible includes the word of God and tells people how to practice their faith and lead good lives. Many people go to church to pray or attend special services, which are usually led by a priest or a minister.

What is Easter?

Easter is a spring festival celebrated by Christians in March or April of every year.

Christians believe that it was on Easter Sunday many years ago that Jesus Christ came back to life. They celebrate this miracle every year during Easter. Jesus Christ is very important for Christians as they believe he is the Son of God.

Sarah says:
GEE-SUS CRY-ST
(Jesus Christ)

Easter is also known as "**Pasch**" or "**Pascha**" in some countries.

The Story of Easter

A long, long time ago in Israel, Jesus Christ came to earth to teach people about the love and goodness of God with the help of his twelve disciples. Jesus healed the sick and performed many miracles.

One of Jesus' disciples, Judas, became very jealous of how loved Jesus was. He decided to betray Jesus to a wicked man called Pontius Pilate, who ruled the land in which Jesus lived. One day, Roman soldiers found Jesus while he was praying and took him away.

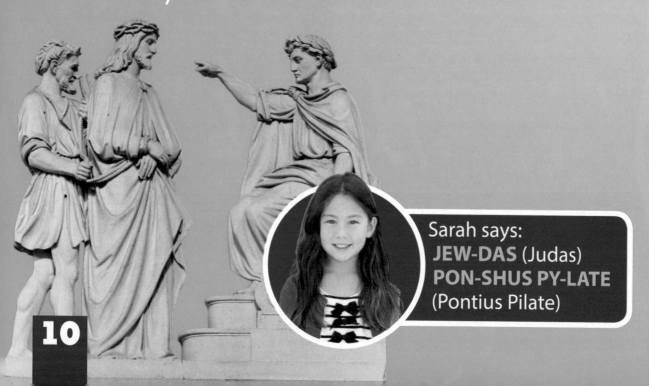

Sarah says:
JEW-DAS (Judas)
PON-SHUS PY-LATE (Pontius Pilate)

That Friday, Pontius Pilate ordered Jesus' hands and feet to be nailed to a cross. Jesus was in great pain for many hours before he died. His body was removed from the cross and placed in a cave with a huge stone covering the entrance.

A few days later, a friend of Jesus, Mary Magdalene, visited the cave. She found, to her surprise, that the huge stone had been moved and that Jesus' body had disappeared. Suddenly, Mary saw Jesus standing outside the cave and Jesus told her that he had returned from the dead. Jesus stayed on Earth for forty days and forty nights before he finally went to heaven to be with God once more.

Good Friday

The Easter festival begins with Good Friday. On Good Friday, Christians remember the day that Jesus was nailed to the cross. Special services are held at church to remember why Jesus died and the love that he had for everyone.

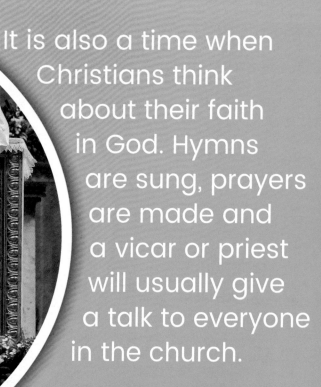

It is also a time when Christians think about their faith in God. Hymns are sung, prayers are made and a vicar or priest will usually give a talk to everyone in the church.

Easter Sunday

Easter Sunday is a joyful day where people celebrate Jesus Christ's return from the dead. Church bells are rung before and after the Easter service and churches are often decorated with candles and spring flowers.

After church, gifts are exchanged, special Easter food is eaten and Christians celebrate their faith in God together with their families and loved ones.

Gifts and Decorations

Easter eggs are often given as gifts during Easter time, as they represent the new life that comes into the world during spring. In many countries, Easter eggs made of chocolate are given as presents.

In the United States, traditional Easter eggs are painted with brightly colored patterns. They are hidden all over the garden for the children to find.

Festive Foods

There are many traditional foods that are eaten at Easter time. Boiled eggs are often eaten for breakfast and roast lamb is usually served for lunch or dinner.

Sweet foods, like simnel cake, are baked at this time of year. Simnel cake is a fruit cake with layers of marzipan in the middle and on top. It is decorated with eleven balls of marzipan to represent Jesus' twelve disciples without Judas.

Sarah says:
SIM-NEL (Simnel)
TWELVE DIS-CY-PLES
(Twelve Disciples)

Family and Friends

Although Christians celebrate their faith in God at Easter time, the festival is also about spending time with family, friends and loved ones.

Families and friends exchange gifts, decorate their homes and enjoy a big feast together to remember this special day.

Sarah Says . . .

Bible
BY-BULL
The Christian holy book containing
the word of God.

Jesus Christ
GEE-SUS CRY-ST
The Son of God.

Judas
JEW-DAS
One of Jesus' twelve disciples, who betrayed him
to Pontius Pilate.

Pontius Pilate
PON-SHUS PY-LATE
The man who ordered Jesus
to be nailed to a cross.

Simnel Cake
SIM-NEL CAKE
A traditional cake made with
marzipan and fruit that is eaten
at Easter.

Twelve Disciples
TWELVE DIS-CY-PLES
The twelve followers
of Jesus Christ.

Log on to www.av2books.com

AV² by Weigl brings you media enhanced books that support active learning. Go to www.av2books.com, and enter the special code found on page 2 of this book. You will gain access to enriched and enhanced content that supplements and complements this book. Content includes video, audio, weblinks, quizzes, a slide show, and activities.

AV² Online Navigation

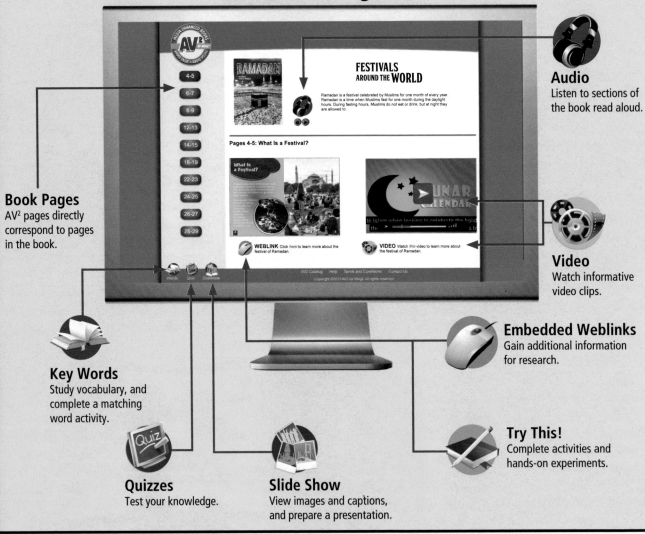

Audio
Listen to sections of the book read aloud.

Book Pages
AV² pages directly correspond to pages in the book.

Video
Watch informative video clips.

Key Words
Study vocabulary, and complete a matching word activity.

Embedded Weblinks
Gain additional information for research.

Try This!
Complete activities and hands-on experiments.

Quizzes
Test your knowledge.

Slide Show
View images and captions, and prepare a presentation.

AV² was built to bridge the gap between print and digital. We encourage you to tell us what you like and what you want to see in the future.

Sign up to be an AV² Ambassador at www.av2books.com/ambassador.